Do Less.
Write More.

The Author's Guide to Finding, Hiring
and Keeping an Excellent Author Assistant

Maria Connor

My Author Concierge

Technology and the virtual marketplace have changed today's publishing industry so that authors, both traditionally and independently published, hold greater accountability for all aspects of their careers, such as product development, design, distribution and marketing. The more time spent on these activities, however, the less time authors have to write.

Author assistants are joining the ensemble of niche publishing support services, like book formatters and publicists. But unlike these service providers, the role and duties of author assistants vary widely. No two author/assistant relationships work the same way or feature the same dynamics. This lack of a consistent, broadly accepted definition is both a challenge and an advantage. The challenge comes in each author having to define what they need from an assistant and how that support will be provided. The advantage is that authors can define and negotiate a support partnership that fits their unique needs and preferences.

Written by the founder of My Author Concierge and professional, full-time author assistant who has worked with more than 50 writers across multiple genres, this guide provides authors with practical, experience-based tips and tools for finding, hiring and keeping an excellent assistant.

Only two duties cannot be delegated by an author to an assistant: writing and reader engagement. Finding the right assistant to help with tasks that can be delegated is one of the smartest business strategies today's authors can utilize. Learn how to *Do Less* in order to *Write More* by finding, hiring and keeping the right author assistant.

Acknowledgements

My gratitude and thanks to the many individuals who generously contributed to this book and to the development of my career as an author assistant. A super-special shout-out to Beth Treadway for suggesting the concept for this guide, and my unending appreciation to Heather Ashby, the first author to say, "Hey, can you take care of this for me?"

Thanks also to Jade Eby, owner and president of The Write Assistants, for sharing the results of her survey of authors about virtual assistants. While this data was collected anonymously and may not offer objective results, this feedback provided helpful insights about some authors' perceptions (negative and positive) of author assistants. Content is used with permission.

I would also like to recognize my fellow author assistants who work passionately and diligently to help authors get their stories in the hands of readers. Whether you call yourself a PA, VA or AA—know that your efforts are appreciated.

Overview

Do Less. Write More is targeted for use by pre-published authors who have never worked with an assistant as well as multi-published authors who rely on an entire team of support individuals. For your convenience, the book has been organized into the following sections:

Introduction 1

What Is an Author Assistant and What Does an Author Assistant Do?... 3

Benefits of Hiring an Author Assistant 9

Determining if You Need an Author Assistant 13

Screening, Interviewing and Hiring an Author Assistant 19

Getting Started with an Author Assistant 27

Real Life Advice 35

About the Author 43

Introduction

When people hear the phrase "romance novel," I suspect a fair number of them picture a classic bodice ripper featuring a windblown Fabio embracing a well-endowed, swooning maiden. Authors and readers of the genre know this is—and has been—a long-outdated stereotype. The same can be said for author assistants.

Five, ten or twenty years ago, only bestselling authors needed, and could afford, assistants. These individuals might more accurately be described as handlers, publicists, secretaries or amanuenses. As a result of changes in the publishing industry, most particularly those influenced by technology, even pre-published authors are finding it beneficial to hire support services, including those of professional assistants who specialize in working with writers.

Unlike many other support services, such as graphic design, audio narration, publicity and editing, there is no single, widely accepted definition for author assistants. This lack of a standardized job description is problematic for a variety of reasons. There are no benchmarks for authors to competitively evaluate and compare skillsets, pricing and methodology. For assistants, it may be difficult to establish professional credibility and value for services when it's a matter of comparing oranges and apples.

Since launching My Author Concierge in 2013, I have seen demand for author assistants increase dramatically. However, the lack of a professional designation often forces authors to hire whomever may be available, without knowing what to expect or how to collaborate with their assistant.

My goal in creating this guide is twofold: To help authors evaluate their needs in order to effectively screen, hire and partner with an assistant, while also educating authors and publishing professionals about the growing number of highly skilled, talented and well educated individuals entering the author assistant market.

It is not my intent to singlehandedly define either the author assistant job description or the author/assistant partnership. I believe the diversity in skills, talents, delivery styles, knowledge and personality is one of the greatest strengths of this particular field. Each assistant offers a unique partnership based on mutual need, temperament, interest, passion and experience. But, as in any relationship, establishing a solid understanding of roles, responsibilities and expectations goes a long way in building a successful, rewarding collaboration.

It is my hope that the compilation of thoughts, suggestions, ideas, tips and strategies offered in *Do Less, Write More* will enable you to find, hire and keep an author assistant who is just right for you.

What Is an Author Assistant and What Does an Author Assistant Do?

In the most general sense, an **author assistant** (AA) is an individual who provides support services to writers on a contract or freelance basis. There are three types of assistants:

Virtual assistant (VA): an individual who works remotely, communicating with authors via email, phone, Skype, etc.

Personal assistant (PA): an individual who works directly (i.e. in person) with the author

Hybrid assistant: an individual who works remotely and directly with an author

In addition to sole proprietor-type assistants, some companies offer author support services. These companies serve as a point of contact, assessing the needs of author clients and then hiring staff or subcontractors to perform the work.

Some assistants work exclusively for a single author while others work with multiple authors. There are advantages and disadvantages to each type of arrangement. Weigh your needs and preferences against the pros and cons to determine what type of assistant is best for you.

Single-client assistant advantages: dedicated support, quicker turnaround, eliminates potential conflict of interest among clients, greater flexibility

Single-client assistant disadvantages: less exposure to strategies used by other authors, may require a certain number of hours per week, a part-time assistant may slow turnaround time

Multi-client assistant advantages: may require less hours (cost shared with other clients), gains knowledge working with a variety of authors, usually works full-time so greater availability, performs tasks more often and thus becomes quicker and more efficient

Multi-client assistant disadvantages: must juggle multiple priorities, require more lead time, less flexibility, potential conflict of interest, perceived "divided" loyalty

One reason it is difficult to standardize the author assistant job description is because the range of services provided by assistants is so broad. *Author assistant* often serves as a catch-all title for anyone who works with authors in some capacity. Some bloggers now offer social media or marketing services to authors, such as organizing and hosting Facebook parties. Some authors compensate avid fans for helping to manage street teams. Many authors hire friends or family members to help with non-writing business tasks such as giveaways or data entry. On occasion, an author may ask someone s/he is already working with—such as a bookkeeper or web designer—to handle additional duties. Each of these individuals may identify themselves as author assistant, as is their right.

It is my opinion, however, that there is a significant difference between a college student who occasionally posts to social media in exchange for spending money and someone who has several years of workforce experience as an executive assistant. There is also a significant difference between that experienced executive assistant and someone with similar credentials who brings publishing expertise to the table.

It is important to realize that not all author assistants are created equal. Some provide very specialized services; some offer a broader skillset. While most individuals can be trained and technical skills can be learned, there is tremendous value in hiring an assistant familiar with your genre and the publishing industry, someone who understands the standards, etiquette, roles, norms, best practices and unwritten rules. The caveat is that a more experienced assistant will garner higher rates.

When it comes to actual tasks and services provided by assistants, it's an open-ended list, dictated by whatever an author needs done. The list below was assembled from a variety of sources, including author assistants' websites, workshop handouts, conference notes and personal experience. Please note some of these services crossover with other support providers such as editors, marketers, graphic designers, website developers, bookkeepers and publicists.

The list is organized according to tasks that require entry level skills, intermediate skills and advanced skills. Note that the execution and mastery of each task will vary, according to skills and experience.

Entry level
Data entry
General office assistance
Mailings
Maintaining schedule
Submitting books to contests
File Maintenance / Organization
Ordering author swag

Intermediate
ARC Distribution
Blog Management
Blog Tour Coordination
Book Club Discussions
Book Signings / Public Appearances (Assist with)
Contest & Giveaway Planning / Management
Coordinate Reviewers / Beta Readers
Correspondence / Mailings
Data Management
Database Management
Managing Street Teams
Newsletter Management / Content
Office Administration
Posting to Social Media/Blog
Research / Fact-checking
Schedule / Travel Coordination
Virtual Party Planning / Hosting

Advanced
Author Branding
Author Education / Consulting
Blog Tour Planning / Management
Book Signings / Public Appearances (Organize and manage)
Copyediting
Cover Copy
Cover Design
Developmental Editing
E-book / Print Formatting
E-book Distribution /Uploading
Event Planning
Ghostwriting
Graphic design
Manuscript Formatting
Marketing / Promotional Campaigns
Media Kits / Media Releases
Merchandizing
Personal Liaison / Point Of Contact
Project Management
Promotional Plan Development
Proofreading
Publicity Liaison
Query Letters
Screening Email / Correspondence
Social Media Content Development / Management
Website Content Creation / Design
Website Development & Maintenance

Again, because of the lack of a standardized job description, rates for author assistants fall across a wide range, depending on experience, skills and duties. Entry level assistants may charge $10-$15 dollars an hour, while advanced assistants charge $35-$50 an hour.

I think it bears mentioning what an author assistant is not or does not do:

- Assistants are not volunteers
- Assistants do not sit around and read all day
- Assistants are not a substitute for other professionals (i.e. editor, financial planner, accountant, contract specialist)
- Assistants are not stand-ins for authors
- Assistants are not (generally) publicists
- Assistants are not privy to a secret formula or magic potion for selling more books, finding more readers or generating more income
- Assistants should not make decisions or commitments on behalf of authors

Benefits of Hiring an Author Assistant

Many authors are intimidated by the thought of hiring an author assistant. There is the cost, not to mention the time and energy required to find, interview, hire and train an assistant. And if things don't work out, you have to repeat the process. It may be tempting to just "do it yourself" because then at least "it will get done right."

Yes, hiring an assistant does require money, time, energy and effort. But finding a great assistant provides many benefits. The value of an outstanding author assistant encompasses not only financial benefits, but non-monetary benefits that are equally important.

- More time to write
- Reduced stress
- Improved organization
- Ability to engage in more opportunities, programs, events, activities
- Handing off tasks you dislike
- Filling your knowledge/experience gap with their knowledge/experience
- Enhance your professional image
- Access to expertise you lack
- Delegation of time-consuming duties
- Marketing knowledge
- Professional connections / networking
- Creativity and new energy
- Consistency and continuity

- More efficient use of your time, resources, energy
- Professionalization of your brand
- Help you clarify goals, priorities
- Expanding your own knowledge base
- Pass along promotional opportunities to you
- Your personal "cheerleader"
- Enjoy a competitive edge
- Coverage for vacations, holidays and sick time

What benefits would be of greatest value to you if you had an author assistant? Jot a list of 5-10 benefits. *Be specific.* If you would like an author assistant to help you become more organized, what does that look like? Are you missing deadlines? Do you want a more structured writing schedule? Is the clutter in your office distracting you from writing? Would you like to have information more readily available, such as a reviewer database?

Taking time to clearly identify your desired benefits will help you prioritize which skills and experience are most important when you begin interviewing candidates. It also enables you to visualize what tasks can be delegated.

A tool commonly used to assess the value of business strategies is a Cost Benefit Analysis. This process entails three steps:

1. Identify and quantify potential risks/costs.

2. Identify and quantify potential benefits/gains.

3. Compare the projected risks and benefits. If the gains exceed the costs, you may want to consider hiring an assistant.

Another, less complex tool to assess the value of this business strategy is to brainstorm a list of pros and cons. Identifying potential drawbacks can help you anticipate and prepare for potential complications in hiring an assistant. For example, if one of the cons is trusting a stranger with confidential information such as user IDs and passwords, possible solutions might include starting out by assigning tasks that don't require confidential information to establish trust or researching if they can be added to your existing account as a user with limited privileges.

Yet another method for assessing the benefit of hiring an assistant is to calculate the value of time gained in words per hour. If you average 600 words per hour when writing, hiring an assistant for five hours a week would allow you to complete an additional 3,000 words per week. If you happen to write 12,000-word novellas, you could potentially complete an additional story every month!

DETERMINING IF YOU NEED AN AUTHOR ASSISTANT

The two most common excuses given by authors as to why they do not hire an assistant is expense ("I can't afford an assistant") and not knowing what tasks to delegate. The third most common excuse is lack of entitlement ("I'm not published yet" or "I only have a few books out").

Other reasons authors may be reluctant to hire an assistant include concerns about reliability and confidentiality, past negative experiences and the potential for mistakes that could damage income/reputation. They may also lack management or business experience and be uncomfortable in a supervisory role.

Let's address the three most common excuses first and then move on to assessing if your career as an author could benefit by hiring an assistant.

I can't afford an assistant.

Publishing high-quality books that will sell and attract readers costs money. As you develop your business plan and budget, consider building in funds for an author assistant. Some assistants are willing to accept project work (such as putting out a monthly newsletter), will work with you on an as-needed basis, allow you to commit to just a couple of hours per month or offer discounts if you purchase blocks of time.

Here's an interesting fact: Many assistants offer a wide variety of skills such as proofreading, ebook formatting, website maintenance and graphic design. While prices for these services vary, you could *save* money by hiring a (qualified) assistant instead of a cover artist or website developer.

For new authors, especially, working with an experienced assistant can save you costly mistakes and prevent embarrassing actions that reflect poorly on your professionalism. If you are new to publishing, consider hiring an assistant to mentor or coach you. Some assistants offer consulting services, which provide authors with resources and how-to knowledge.

I'm not published yet/only have a few books out.

The most effective strategy for establishing your author career is to write more books. Both traditionally and self-published authors hold accountability for non-writing related tasks, such as accounting, marketing, advertising and engaging with readers. While full-time writers have 40-60 hours per week to dedicated to all career-related tasks, many authors work full or part-time "day jobs." Add in family obligations, health issues, commute time, college classes, travel, etc., and you see how the time available to actually write quickly dwindles.

Delegating one or two labor-intensive, non-writing tasks to an assistant can free up more time to write. More writing equals more books. More books equal more sales. The key to making this type of investment pay-off is to carefully evaluate how much time you are applying to non-writing related tasks and what tasks you can afford to hire out. Using the 80/20 rule is one method to identify decisions that will lead to more effective management of your resources: time, energy, creativity, and money. According to this adage, 20 percent of your activities generate 80 percent of your income. They key is to minimize how much time you spend on activities that don't generate income and focus instead where the pay-off is greatest.

I don't know what to do with an assistant.

Many authors, particularly self-published authors, are control freaks and perfectionists. That's one reason many choose to self-publish in the first place. However, these traits can inhibit your career growth and undermine goal achievement. The reluctance to delegate tasks to an assistant is often rooted in fear, distrust and uncertainty. Will the assistant perform the task correctly? Will the assistant meet deadlines? Is the assistant really as skilled as s/he claims?

There are strategies to overcome these concerns (see the section *Getting Started with an Author Assistant*), but the first step in overcoming this objection is educating yourself about author assistants. Learn how other authors and assistants work together. Ask what kinds of tasks your peers delegate to their support staff. Attend workshops given by author assistants to become acquainted with the attitude, personality and conduct of these professionals. Lastly, realize that developing an working partnership with an assistant is just like any other relationship; it takes time to build trust, rapport and empathy.

Once you've opened yourself to the possibility that hiring an author assistant can be a positive, productive experience, the next step is determining if you need an author assistant. If you aren't sure, try one of these assessments.

Track your time for two or three days.

Determine how much time you spend on every single task. Be honest and be accurate. A summary that reveals you frequently interrupt your writing to check Facebook may indicate a need to either organize, limit or delegate your social media activity. You may also be surprised to see how many non-writing tasks you handle on a daily basis. Using an Excel spreadsheet or Word document table is a simple way to organize this information.

Professional self-assessment.

Answer these questions. The responses may indicate areas where you need help.

- Are you meeting your writing goals and deadlines?
- Is your social media regularly updated?
- Do you avoid tasks because you dislike and/or lack the ability to perform them?
- Are you losing writing time to repetitive, basic tasks?
- Do you procrastinate to avoid certain tasks?
- Is your creativity and/or productivity suffering because you feel overwhelmed?
- Do you feel like you are working harder than ever but not making progress?

- Are you losing writing time trying to figure out how to perform certain tasks?
- Do you want to expand your career and/or grow your readership?
- Are you turning down opportunities because you're too busy?
- Do you need better work/life balance?
- Are you disorganized and unproductive?
- Are your personal work relationships suffering (i.e. working with spouse, friend, family member)?
- Have you taken a vacation (a *real* vacation) in the last three years?

These assessments, much like the exercises designed to recognize the benefits of hiring an author assistant, can be useful in preparing yourself for success in hiring and working with an assistant by defining what tasks you wish to delegate and what skills are needed to perform these assignments.

While there are many reasons to hire an assistant, there are also indicators that now might not be the right time to recruit assistance.

- Are you fully committed to a publishing career?
- Do you have clearly defined career and production goals?
- Can you afford to hire a *qualified, experienced, knowledgeable* author assistant?
- Do you know where you need help?
- Are you prepared to invest the time, energy and effort required into building a partnership with an assistant?

Screening, Interviewing and Hiring an Author Assistant

Before You Start

Before you start looking for a virtual assistant, and especially before you hire someone, make sure you have a general idea about what you want from an assistant. Take time to answer these questions:

- What services do you need? Prioritize your list, especially if financial resources are limited.
- How much can you afford to pay an assistant? Per hour? Per week? Per month?
- What skills, experience and/or knowledge are mandatory? Desirable? A nice bonus?
- What type of working relationship do you prefer (virtual or in-person)?
- Do you want a dedicated assistant or one who handles multiple clients?
- What is your preferred method of communication? Email, Skype, phone?
- What type of availability do you desire? Monday through Friday? Holidays? Evenings? Weekends?
- What qualities do you value in a person? Don't overlook the importance of compatibility.
- Do you have any special considerations, needs or requirements? For example, do you write erotica? Do you require someone who can be on-call? Do you work with overseas vendors?

Plan ahead. Evaluate your production schedule to determine when you need help. Allow yourself sufficient lead time to recruit, hire and train an assistant.

Consult with an accountant, tax advisor or lawyer about hiring practices and issues, such as filing state/federal documentation, reporting salary payouts, and so forth. There may be different implications if you hire a firm versus an individual.

Finding Potential Author Assistants

Approach your search for an author assistant the same way you would look for an agent, editor or publisher. Use a variety of sources to generate a solid list of potential candidates. Don't worry about having too many leads, as some assistants will not meet your criteria and some will not be accepting clients. Use these strategies to locate and assemble a list of author assistants:

- Ask friends and business peers for recommendations and referrals.
- Ask to be introduced to assistants at events and/or conferences.
- Attend workshops given by author assistants.
- Post your request in professional/author groups you belong to.
- Do an online search
- Check out referral sites such as Author's Atlas and Author EMS
- Check out sites for freelancers such as Upwork and Freelancer

- If you query an assistant and learn they are not available, always ask them for recommendations.
- Even if an assistant seem not to be a match, save the information for future reference.
- Visit assistants' websites, even for those individuals you do not intend to interview, just to get an idea of rates, services, skills and clientele.
- Organize your information in a spreadsheet or document so you can make notes and comments, and track your queries.

The topic of training and certification is fuzzy when it comes to author assistants. Author's Assistants (http://authorsassistants.com/) offers two levels of certification for Professional Virtual Author's Assistants and describes its course as "the world's only training program to teach virtual professionals to work with authors." It is reasonable to expect that other individuals and businesses will develop training materials and/or programs targeted at author assistants given the increased demand for such services. **A word of caution to both authors and individuals considering a career as an author assistant: Be discerning when it comes to the value and credibility of *certifications*.** The lack of a regulating organization, disparity in roles and duties, and ongoing evolution of this profession make it difficult to establish industry-wide standards for career certification.

It is not uncommon for authors to hire family members, friends or fans/readers as assistants. While these collaborations can be successful, there is potential for trouble. A few things to consider:

- How will you address problems/concerns?
- If the arrangement does not work out, how might it affect the original relationship?
- Services provided by a "hobbyist" or volunteer assistant may be inconsistent, sporadic or unreliable.
- Does this individual have the skills, knowledge and ability to perform the job in a professional capacity?
- Compensating a fan or reader with free books or gift cards is not the same thing as paying for professional services.

Screening and Interviewing Author Assistants

Once you have a list of potential author assistants, start by screening and researching each candidate. The best places to start are their websites, blogs, social media profiles and LinkedIn profiles. While reviewing these sources, keep these questions and considerations in mind:

- What is their background? What qualifies them to be a professional author assistant?
- Do they have experience in the publishing industry?
- Is their online presence professional?
- How strong are their writing skills?
- Are reviews and/or recommendations listed?
- How long have they been in business?

Before inviting candidates to participate in an interview, prepare a job description or list of duties. Based on these criteria, you can then develop a list of interview questions.

The first step in the interview process is to query author assistants via email. Compose a friendly email with a brief introduction, where you learned about them and a request for more information. Be sure to include your contact information, website and any special considerations. The responses you receive will help you refine your master list of candidates based on availability, first impression and compatibility.

When it comes to interviewing assistants, consider a face-to-face meeting, telephone call or video chat. This allows you to personally engage with the individual and offers the opportunity to evaluate personality, professional conduct and non-verbal signals. In addition to your own list of interview questions, here are other prompts that may be helpful.

- How long have you worked as an author assistant?
- How did you get started as an author assistant?
- Share a few examples of tasks/services you perform for other authors.
- What do you most enjoy about being an author assistant?
- What do you know about me and my books?
- What is your experience in the publishing industry?
- What specific skills, education, credentials, abilities or experience do you offer?
- What technical programs and applications are you skilled in?
- What is your work schedule/availability?
- What is the average turnaround time for assignments?

- How would you handle this situation (*describe scenario such as missed deadline, error, disgruntled reader*)?
- Please provide a work sample (*i.e. newsletter, social media content, formatting, editing*).
- What is your backup plan in the event you have a personal emergency or become unavailable?
- What are your prices and how do you handle billing/payment?
- Do you have a contract (*request a copy*)?
- Please provide me with the names of past or current clients.

Hiring an Author Assistant

Once you are ready to hire an assistant, prepare a job offer. Include total hours, compensation and duties to be performed OR services to be provided. Some assistants may provide a contract while others are comfortable with less formal documentation. **It is in both parties' best interests to have a signed agreement.**

Consider having the author assistant sign a non-disclosure agreement (also known as a confidentiality agreement). Samples of basic service contracts and NDAs are available on the internet.

You may want to propose a trial arrangement, such as three months or a set number of hours. This allows you to evaluate the working relationship, job performance and value of hiring an assistant without making a long-term commitment.

As mentioned previously, consult with an accountant, tax advisor or lawyer for state and federal employment requirements, tax forms and reporting payments made to independent contractors.

Getting Started with an Author Assistant

Congratulations! You have found and hired an author assistant. Now comes the hard part—negotiating a new relationship.

Whether you have hired a business to provide assistance with tasks and projects or an individual, as in any partnership, both parties have rights and responsibilities.

Author Rights and Responsibilities

You have the right to expect that work will be done accurately and in a timely fashion.

You have the right to request documentation of completed work, such as receipts, email exchanges, etc.

You have the right to ask that work be corrected or re-done if it does not meet standards and specifications.

You have the right for final approval of any work completed/submitted on your behalf.

You have the right to require that work be done according to your methods and procedures.

You have the right to expect courteous, professional conduct.

You are responsible for providing timely, constructive feedback on work completed.

You are responsible for providing the materials, resources and information needed for work to be completed as requested.

You are responsible for providing guidance and clear directives.

You are responsible for clearly communicating deadlines.

You are responsible for determining boundaries and realistic expectations.

Author Assistant Rights and Responsibilities

You have the right to expect courteous, professional conduct.

You have the right to request clarification and guidance for work assigned to you.

You have the right to request that payment for materials, supplies, software, etc. necessary to perform your job will be paid for and provided by the hiring author.

You have the right to set regular work hours and respond to communications in a timely fashion based on that schedule.

You have the right to be compensated for business-related expenses such as travel, hotel, meals, event registration, etc. if required and approved by the hiring author, unless other terms are negotiated.

You are responsible for accurate and timely completion of work.

You are responsible for notifying the author of any problems, complications or circumstances that impact your ability to complete or perform tasks.

You are responsible for representing the author in a courteous and professional manner at all times, both online and in person.

You are responsible for protecting the author's interests (financial, material, reputation, etc.) at all times.

You are responsible for actively supporting the author's success by showing initiative, proposing ideas and solving problems.

How to Negotiate and Establish a Successful Working Relationship

Once you've hired an assistant, you may feel nervous, apprehensive, excited and/or relieved. Emotions and personality may influence the author/assistant partnership, so approach the venture with optimism, enthusiasm and positivity. Pay attention to the needs, preferences and quirks of your assistant and make sure s/he is aware of yours as well. Here are some tips and suggestions for launching strong.

Understand that, like any new relationship, it will take time to develop trust and a degree of comfort in working with your assistant.

Be fair and respectful when communicating problems, concerns, preferences, dislikes and annoyances.

Provide clear expectations, instructions and well-defined deliverables. Samples, examples, written guidelines and a well-defined final product will insure your expectations are met the first time.

Communicate time-sensitive projects and deadlines by flagging dates in emails and communications.

Schedule daily/weekly status checks, via phone or email.

Offer timely and frequent constructive feedback and praise for a job well done.

Be familiar with the tasks assigned so you know the steps involved and average turnaround time.

Pad deadlines to build in time for corrections, modifications or—worst case scenario—outsourcing to someone else.

Establish clear boundaries. What actions/decisions are your assistant authorized to make?

Avoid last-minute requests. This creates potential for errors, mistakes, shoddy workmanship, as well as stress and frustration.

Begin by delegating one or two non-critical tasks. This is a good way to get acquainted, learn each other's working style, assess strengths and challenges, and build trust.

Provide copies of your books so your assistant can read and be familiar with your work.

Set up the Right Tools and Technology

Working with a virtual assistant requires a different approach to collaboration and communicating. Consider how you prefer to share information, files and materials. Investigate options for organizing and communicating projects. Many authors and assistants find these applications useful:

Dropbox (file sharing)
Google Drive (file sharing)
Google Chat (communications/meeting)
Skype (communications/meeting, screen sharing)
Google Calendar (scheduling)
Basecamp (task/project management)
Asana (task/project management)
Trello (task/project management)
Snagit (image and video screen capture)
Yammer (communication platform

Training an Author Assistant

Even the most experienced author assistant will require some degree of training and orientation. There are several ways to achieve this, including written instructions, providing examples and samples, developing a procedure manual, and/or using audio/video (web cam, screen captures, screen sharing, and videos).

Training and/or reference materials may include website/account logon information; book database;

series bibles; names and contact information for vendors, reviewers, cross-promotion partners; book files; graphics; media kit; etc.

The most important elements for fast and efficient training are detailed instructions and clearly defined outcomes/deliverables. Check in with your assistant at various stages of a project or assignment to determine if additional information is needed and insure requirements are being met.

Starter Tasks and Projects

Getting started isn't always easy. What job should you assign first? Look at tasks you dislike or avoid, or projects you've had to shelve for lack of time. Here are a few suggestions to help find a starting point:

- Organize, collect, research and/or assemble data, such as reviews, bloggers, advertisers, or buy links for each book.
- Develop a production schedule or To Do List with daily, weekly, monthly tasks.
- Ask your assistant to draft content for your review (i.e. social media posts, newsletter content, teasers).
- Mailing out author swag or giveaways.
- Review website, social media profiles and vendor listings to make sure content is complete and up-to-date.

Working through Problems

While careful planning and due diligence can prevent many problems, issues may arise as you settle into this new working relationship. It is important to remain respectful and courteous, but flexibility, patience and a commitment to resolving the issue are paramount. If difficulties arise, these strategies may help:

- Speak up as soon as you sense things are headed in the wrong direction
- Give your assistant an opportunity to correct the error or fix the problem
- State what needs to be done to resolve the problem
- Ask what happened to identify actions to prevent the problem from reoccurring
- Continue to demonstrate faith and trust after an error has been made

Not all author/assistant partnerships work out, for a variety of reasons. It may be due—on both sides—to poorly matched skills, a lack of required skills, poor communication, unrealistic expectations, incompatibility, decreased availability, a change in circumstance or personal factors. If it becomes necessary to terminate services, provide advance notice (if possible and appropriate) and be professional. Ask for a final summary of hours and fees owed, as well as status on outstanding/incomplete projects/tasks. In the event an assistant chooses to discontinue working for you, don't take it personally.

Remember, when starting out with a new assistant, make sure you allow plenty of time for onboarding. Be available to answer questions or provide feedback. Professional assistants are ready, willing and able to meet the needs and expectations of author clients, given the opportunity to do so.

Real Life Advice

This section includes practical tips, suggestions, insights and strategies from authors and author assistants.

Author Note: Comments are not attributed to source in order to preserve confidentiality and encourage candor.

The first thing I did was sat down and really thought about what I needed help with. Was it just a street team? Some blog tours? Graphics here and there? Everything under the sun? The answer to that question really drove my search. From there I Googled a lot, hunted authors that were very popular and mentioned they used assistants. I poured through blogs that had occasional guest posts from assistants, and generally delved into the VA world. I even found a couple of virtual assistant-only forums where other assistants spoke about what they did for authors and coached others. I approached searching for an assistant in the same way I approach research for my books. I was focused on finding out everything I could. Does that mean I didn't make mistakes? Hell no! I went through five--FIVE--assistants before I finally found one that I could work with, was willing to learn my crazy quirks and handled all of my deadlines.

One thing I would recommend is keeping your initial budget with each assistant smaller. If they charge an hourly rate, start with a handful of hours, see what they can accomplish for you in that time. Make sure what they do accomplish is right before you start giving them more responsibilities. It really hurts the pocket to contract twenty hours only to realize after five hours that the relationship just isn't going to work.

One thing to remember is that not everyone is good at everything. You need to be clear on your expectations and either hunt for someone who can meet them ALL or be willing to work with someone who can give you 80 percent of what you need and maybe look for someone else to handle that last 20 percent. I know several authors who have more than one person working with them simply because they find assistants that do one thing really, really well and that's all they need from that person.

Know your strengths and weaknesses in the business (I'm technically challenged and don't want to take time away from my writing to learn it just yet or maybe ever).

Know what you are looking for in an assistant.

Know your budget (dollar and hour).

Pay attention to your gut instinct. Do you feel you can trust this assistant with your account numbers, passwords, etc.? If not, move on; this person isn't the one for you.

Take time to research on loops and find out what other authors are saying about assistants, the authors' needs and what duties they need in an assistant

Make sure your contract has a confidentiality and an "out" clause.

Don't settle for just anyone because you're overwhelmed or should have hired an assistant ages ago. A bad assistant is worse than no assistant.

Comparison shop. How much does each assistant charge? But don't take the least expensive one; hire the assistant who fits most of your needs and you feel most comfortable dealing with.

Consider the assistant's link to the book industry. If they are on the "fringes," they may not know the industry lingo and you may have to take time to teach them the ropes.

Ask how long they have been an assistant and for examples of their work, such as author newsletters, ads they've created, Facebook or Twitter banners, etc.

The use of a shared calendar is really helpful versus long lists in emails.

Check-in phone calls are helpful.

Prioritize projects and assign deadlines.

Learn your assistant's strengths and maximize those skills.

Consider dividing your work between two assistants. This enhances coverage and compliments skillsets.

More and more authors, especially indie authors, are building support teams comprised of specialists such as editors and graphic designers. Finding the right assistant can round out this team and make life a lot easier.

You cannot assume your assistant will know 1) what you want done, 2) when you want it done, and 3) how you want it done. COMMUNICATE!

The front-end investment of developing training materials creates resources that you can use if you need to hire another assistant or add staff.

Characteristics of a good author assistant:

- Someone organized
- Someone on top of things/covers the bases
- Smart
- Learns quickly
- Takes on jobs, learns, and exceeds—goes the extra mile
- Knows the business
- Can go with the flow/adapt/change easily
- Willing to learn and take direction
- Willing to listen
- Tech knowledge/savvy/website knowledge

Warning signs of a poor author assistant:

- Does not take direction well
- Questions authority or refuses to follow instructions
- Gives unsolicited, contradictory advice
- Poor workmanship
- Execution doesn't align with stated skills
- Overstepping boundaries/authority

If after you're working together, you are not on the same page or don't seem to click, it's best to go your separate ways rather than have a relationship riddled with aggravation and frustration. The same is true for the assistant. If s/he is finding it difficult to work with you, you're better off taking her/his suggestion that you find someone else. Having an assistant is supposed to help you, not make your working life more difficult.

Decide ahead of time what it is you want an assistant to do. Is it important for you to meet face to face on a regular basis, or are emails and phone conversations enough for you? Are you looking for someone to just do a few things on a hit and miss basis, or do you need continuous support? How comfortable are you with sharing things like bank account information, PayPal information, passwords, etc. on your various accounts? Is your potential assistant comfortable having that information?

Unless your assistant only works for you, don't expect an immediate response to your every request. A good assistant will be able to go quickly through emails and sort them according to priority. Sometimes your request is not as important as another client's, but a good assistant knows the difference.

Consider what you want in an author assistant. Do you want someone who will only complete requested tasks or someone who will also brainstorm with you, share ideas, back you up when you're in the trenches and take the initiative? It's important to be clear about the expectations up front.

Recognize the value of industry knowledge, professionalism and connections. You can't be everywhere at once. An assistant who actively participates in groups, conferences, seminars, etc., can fill you in on what you're missing and suggest resources.

Observe how the person conducts her/himself, especially on social media. Choose someone who's in line with your platform and image. They represent you.

If you're a new author, making a monthly or even quarterly commitment may not make sense. Consider an assistant with a reasonable hourly rate or if they don't have an hourly rate listed, see if you can negotiate a workable fee. They may be willing to work with you.

Communicate and have a plan. It's helpful for your assistant to understand you, your platform, career plans, as well as the expectations of your agent, publicist, publisher, etc. Consider your author assistant as a team member. The more they know ahead of time, the better they can support you.

Don't forget assistants have other clients and commitments to balance along with your needs. They also have a life outside of their work.

Remember that many author assistants are driven by the same passion for publishing and storytelling that inspires you as a writer. They do this work because they love it.

Don't forget to say thank you and let them know how much you appreciate them! They free up time for you to create and live your dream.

About the Author

Maria Connor is an award-winning journalist and author with more than 15 years' experience in the publishing industry. In 2013 she launched My Author Concierge, which provides marketing, editorial, technical and administrative support services to authors, primarily in the romantic fiction genre. Since then, she has worked with more than 50 authors across multiple genres. A frequent workshop presenter at national and regional conferences, she is actively engaged in helping authors achieve career goals through education, advocacy and mentoring. Visit MyAuthorConcierge.com for more information.

COPYRIGHT

Published by Maria Connor. Do Less. Write More. Copyright © 2015 Maria Connor. ALL RIGHTS RESERVED. This book contains material protected under International and Federal Copyright Laws and Treaties. Any unauthorized reprint or use of this material is prohibited. No part of this book may be reproduced or transmitted in any form or by any means, electronic or mechanical, including photocopying, recording, or by any information storage and retrieval system without express written permission from the author.

Made in the USA
Lexington, KY
09 February 2018